The Dexter Cider Mill Apple Cookbook

Enjoy!
Katherine Koziski

Katherine Merkel Koziski

Cheri Smith
Food Photographer

Andrew Sacks
Photographer

Katherine Merkel Koziski
Food Stylist

A portion of the proceeds
of this book will be donated to the
Breast Cancer Research Program
of the Michigan Cancer Foundation

This cookbook is a collection of favorite recipes,
which are not necessarily original recipes.

Library of Congress Catalog Number: 95-60312
ISBN: 0-87197-427-4

Edited, Designed and Manufactured by
Favorite Recipes® Press
P.O. Box 305142
Nashville, Tennessee 37230
1-800-358-0560

Manufactured in the United States of America
First Printing: 1995 15,000 copies

DEDICATION

To our four daughters, their spouses and our grandchildren for their patience during the time I spent preparing this cookbook

To my husband, especially, for his historical and technical contribution to this book, and his continual encouragement

IN APPRECIATION

To Cheri Smith for her sense of humor, encouragement and talent in bringing the manuscript to life in photography

To Merkel Home Furnishings, Inc. and Glenbrier Antiques and Fireside Antiques for allowing me to borrow accessories for the food photographs

To the Michigan Apple Committee for their apple information and endorsement of this cookbook

PREFACE

As a child, my first recollections of wonderful food were at my Grandmother Merkel's home. She would stand in her kitchen and beat butter and sugar together with a wooden spoon until it was light and fluffy for her oatmeal raisin cookies. No high-powered mixers would have been used in her kitchen, even if they had been available. Most of her cakes and cookies were made with hickory nuts, a delectable nut that we rarely use today, and, of course, sweet butter. She would make sweet yeast bread and turn it into flat sheets for a coffeecake and smother it with "real" heavy cream, brown sugar, and cinnamon. The remainder of the dough was cut into strips and fried, then dusted with confectioners' sugar for what we called "long Johns." Later our family shared summer cottages side by side with my aunt and uncle. I spent many hours in Aunt Mary's kitchen watching her mix, roll, cut, and fry doughnuts.

She would let me sugar them, which was a great privilege, since she didn't allow just anyone in her kitchen. She taught me how to make my first chocolate cake from scratch and the frosting was of her own invention — no recipe, of course, just her eye for just the right amount of chocolate and confectioners' sugar. I regret that at the time I was too young to have taken notes of all of this wonderful baking. Throughout the years, however, my family has given me handwritten books by both my grandmother and aunt containing their brief notes on some of their recipes. During high school, I took every Home Economics class offered, even the sewing, which I disliked, but which was required. Our instructor was a role model for me in the way she presented the course, and I subsequently

went on to major in foods and nutrition in college.
After college, I spent a few years in the test kitchen of the Kellogg Company. At Kellogg's, I was responsible for developing recipes using cereal as an ingredient. The job was not only fun, but I gained valuable experience in the food business.
Since then I have spent more that thirty years as a wife and the mother of four daughters, transferring around the country with a corporate husband. We finally settled in Michigan and I took a corporate position. During a few of those years, I was a cancer patient, but, thankfully, have been in remission for several years now.
When we purchased the Cider Mill, our lives were still very filled with our corporate jobs and the weekend operation of the Mill during the autumn months. Now retired and with more time to devote to this project, I launched into the testing and photography for this book. Even though I have a background in foods and nutrition, writing a cookbook is not something hastily done. The project has been in my head, in my kitchen, and on my word processor for over two years.
Although you must follow instructions for the actual preparation of these tested recipes, your imagination is given free rein to experiment with different varieties of apples, adding or deleting a spice or seasoning. Every recipe is designed for the home cook; all ingredients are readily obtainable from most supermarkets. Even the necessary baking utensils are stocked at any well-equipped cookware shop or department store.
If you do not have a cider mill or orchard nearby, you can find many apple varieties and apple cider all year long in your local grocery or produce store.
I hope you will enjoy this cookbook as much as I have enjoyed putting it together, and may your imagination soar with the limitless possibilities of "cooking with apples."

CONTENTS

Main Dishes

Desserts

APPLES — YESTERDAY AND TODAY

We would like to share with you some interesting historical information and facts regarding apples. To begin with, apples are a member of the rose family, as are pears, peaches, cherries, plums and raspberries. Although apples were indigenous to America, they were more like crabapples and unlike the apples we know today, which were brought by English settlers in the early 1600s. The first apple orchard was started shortly thereafter in Boston, Massachusetts. It probably contained some of the old varieties we can still find today, such as the Roxbury Russet or the Westfield-Seek-No-Further — great names for apples. Henry Ward Beecher, a well-known preacher in the 1800s, once stated that, "there is pleasure in having a decorous name to a great fruit." This same feeling is with us today, with new varieties such as Imperial Gala and Golden Delicious. John Chapman, a prominent apple personality who was also known as Johnny Appleseed, was born in Massachusetts in 1774 and went west following another generation of settlers, planting apple trees along the way. During the 1820s, apple seeds were planted as far west as the present state of Washington, which is now the largest producer of apples in the United States. As the state of Michigan was being settled, many families brought apple stock from the Eastern states or directly from Europe. This has resulted not only in the availability of many varieties reflecting the personal tastes and needs of these families, but also in the expanding market of that time and today. Known as the "Variety State", Michigan is fortunate to have the type of climate that provides cool nights to build flavor, sunlight for color, and rain to swell the apple. The Great Lakes help delay fruit bloom, which lessens the possibility of freeze damage to apple blossoms in the spring.

The development of an apple has some interesting characteristics worth noting. For example, apple flowers usually grow in groups of five. Whereas most apple blossoms are pink at first, they turn back to white. Interestingly, the seeds from an apple do not bear true to the apple from which they came. Instead apples varieties are propagated by grafting. To develop a new apple variety is a long process, from twenty to forty years or longer.

In the area of good health, there are a number of worthy aspects to apples which bear noting. Most of us have heard the expression that "eating an apple a day keeps the doctor away." A less commonly known version from the middle ages is that "eating an apple before going to bed makes the doctor beg his bread." These seem to bear some truth when you understand the value that apples provide to us. To name a few:

The skin of an apple contains fiber which is important to our digestive system.

Apples are cholesterol free. The pectin in an apple actually reduces cholesterol levels.

Apples are low in sodium and rich in potassium, Vitamins A, B-1, B-2, C and E, which is important for the heart.

Apples are considered nature's toothbrush, in that they make our teeth feel clean and shiny.

Some apples have unique characteristics when it comes to consuming them either by baking them or by eating them raw. The Northern Spy is a wonderful baking apple; its flavor and firmness hold up extremely well. The Jonathan apple, long popular throughout the area, produces a pink applesauce. The Cortland is often used in salads because it does not readily turn an unappetizing brown.Yellow Delicious and Criterian have the same characteristics.

Your personal cooking enthusiasm and sense of culinary adventure can lead you to similar findings among many of the apple varieties long appreciated by our forefathers, but somewhat diminished in popularity by today's marketing need to produce apples of durable and high yield varieties. They are out there, but you need to seek them out.

ABOUT THE MILL

The "pressing" business of making cider started at the Dexter Cider Mill in 1886 by Mr. Tuttle and Mr. Van Ettan, a Civil War Veteran.

The Mill is located in Dexter, Michigan, just a short distance from Ann Arbor, on the banks of the Huron River. Its design was typical for cider mills of that era, with two stories. The top story was for receiving the apples, washing them, and grinding them into pomace or mash ready for pressing. The pomace was gravity fed and assembled for the press on the lower floor. Because the Mill was built into the side of a river bank, natural refrigeration was available to keep the cider cool. The proximity to the river also provided two additional benefits: the first benefit was power, first for a wheel and then steam, which has since been converted to electricity. The second benefit allowed for the disposal of the pomace, which is no longer done.

The Mill was purchased in the early 1900s by Otto Wagner; he and his son Fred and family made cider for 86 years before the Mill was purchased by the Koziski family. We believe that so few owners over all these years has preserved the Mill and the cider-making process for our current customers and their children to observe and appreciate. We are proud to be able to preserve a piece of history to share with our many world-class customers.

THE MAKING OF CIDER

Now to the subject of making good cider, which takes planning. The cider maker must be familiar with apple varieties that are high in sugar, such as Red and Golden Delicious and even less well known cider varieties such as Winter Banana. He combines approximately 30% of these types of apples with 50 % to 60% of apples that are high in acid, such as Jonathans, Cortlands, McIntosh, Rome Beauty, or Northern Spy. The presence of acid cleanses the palate, creating a crisp and smooth, but not syrupy, cider. Finally, he adds a small percentage, about 10%, of apples that will give the cider an aroma or bouquet. McIntosh, Red Delicious and Winter Banana give the cider a pleasing bouquet.

We find that in some years, apple varieties will change, becoming sweeter or less acidic than the previous year. We always taste the apples before beginning a press in order to adjust the blend. One of the aspects of producing a blended cider is its uniqueness. By combining various varieties, we can produce a taste totally unique to one that cannot be duplicated by eating any one apple. This can lead to producing cider of interesting tastes, using varieties not often available, such as Baldwin, Rhode Island Greenings or Snow apples.

Finally, we always use ripe apples, which will give the best flavor and highest yield. You can determine if an apple is ripe by cutting it open. If the seeds are brown, it is ripe; if they are white, it is not.

Once we have selected the apples and have established the blend, we start the process by washing and brushing the apples, and forcing them into a centrifugal shredder. This reduces the apples to a mash or pomace, which as mentioned earlier,

is gravity fed, five bushels or 200 pounds at a time, into the press room (left), where it is captured on 6- by 6-foot press cloths of high strength material laid across a form which is 40 by 40 inches square and 6 inches deep (below). The corners of the press cloth are then folded into the center of the form, creating an envelope of pomace (right, below). The form is removed and a 45- by 45-inch oak rack is laid on top of the press cloth. The form is then laid on top of the next oak rack and another press cloth is placed across the form, ready for the next 200 pounds of apples.
This process is repeated seven times, totaling 35 to 40 bushels of apples, or approximately 1500 pounds. The press cart is then rolled into the press. The electric motor is started, which drives a number of large belts off a long drive shaft. One belt drives a set of pistons which compresses hydraulic fluid, forcing a

twelve-inch diameter piston to ram the rack against the press bulkhead, releasing the cider from the apple pomace (right). Since an apple can give up as much as 80% of its volume in juice, the yield is approximately 100 gallons of cider with each press. The cider is suctioned off into a refrigerated tank, and from there it is sold.

The entire process takes approximately one hour. Again, this is the same process that has been used for over 100 years at the Dexter Cider Mill, providing many families in the vicinity with delicious juice.

We are often asked what is the difference between commercial apple juice and cider. Typically, commercial apple juice is pasteurized and, as a result, will not ferment. It is also highly filtered, and sometimes has preservatives added. Fresh cider, with no preservatives, will ferment.

BEVERAGES

BUTTERED APPLE GROG

Ingredients

2 tablespoons Calvados
or apple brandy
1/4 cup apple cider
2 tablespoons dry vermouth
2 whole cloves
1 slice peeled apple
1 teaspoon butter
1 lemon slice
Sugar to taste

Serves One

This recipe for Buttered Apple Grog makes one serving, but it can easily be increased for the number you wish to serve. Calvados is an apple brandy available in most liquor stores.

Directions

Combine the Calvados, apple cider, wine and cloves in a medium saucepan. Cook until heated through but not boiling. Place the apple slice, butter and lemon slice in an old-fashioned glass or coffee mug. Add sugar to taste. Pour the hot grog into the glass, stirring to melt the butter and dissolve the sugar. Serve immediately.

Braeburn

Braeburn is a new apple variety that originated as a chance seedling in New Zealand. It is a medium to large apple with a gold-green base shaded by striping red color. The flesh is crisp, very juicy, full-flavored and mildly sweet. It is a late season apple with a long storage life.

CRANBERRY AND APPLE PUNCH

Ingredients

Cranberry ice cubes
1 quart cranberry juice cocktail, chilled
3 cups apple cider, chilled
2 cups club soda, chilled
1/2 cup fresh lemon juice

Garnish

1 orange, thinly sliced
1 lemon, thinly sliced

Serves Eighteen

This recipe will satisfy our many requests for a nonalcoholic punch. The color is crimson and the garnish adds color. Freeze a quart of cider in the autumn months so you will be able to make this punch during the holiday season. Add cranberry ice cubes made from cranberry juice cocktail frozen in two ice cube trays.

Directions

Place the cranberry ice cubes in a 3 1/2-quart punch bowl or pitcher. Add the cranberry juice, apple cider, club soda and lemon juice; stir gently to mix well. Garnish with the orange and lemon slices.

Crispin (Mutsu)

The Crispin, a cross between the Golden Delicious and Indo varieties, is a relatively newer apple variety being grown in limited numbers. It was discovered in Japan in 1930, and originally named Mutsu. It was renamed Crispin in the United Kingdom in 1968. The Crispin is shaped much like the Golden Delicious, and is larger in size than many other varieties. It is green in color, with pale creamy white flesh. It has a firm, fine textured and juicy flesh, with a slightly sweet, refreshing and moderate flavor.

MULLED CIDER

Ingredients

2 quarts apple cider
1 orange, sliced
1 lemon, sliced
4 cinnamon sticks
6 whole cloves
1/4 teaspoon ground nutmeg
1/4 teaspoon ground ginger

Garnish

Orange and lemon slices
Cinnamon sticks

Serves Sixteen

The word "mull" means to flavor a beverage by heating it with various ingredients such as herbs, spices, fruit and sugar. The beverages most often infused in this fashion are wine, cider and beer. Our recipes, of course, use apple cider.

Directions

Combine the apple cider, orange slices, lemon slices, cinnamon, cloves, nutmeg and ginger in a 3-quart saucepan. Bring to a boil and reduce the heat to low. Simmer for 30 to 40 minutes. Strain into mugs. Garnish servings with additional orange or lemon slices and a cinnamon stick stirrer.

HOT CRANBERRY CIDER

Ingredients

1 quart apple cider
2 cups cranberry juice cocktail
1 teaspoon whole cloves
1 cinnamon stick

Serves Six to Eight

Hot Cranberry Cider is quick and easy to prepare when you arrive home from a winter skating or sledding party.

Directions

Combine the apple cider, cranberry juice cocktail, cloves and cinnamon in a large saucepan. Bring to a boil and reduce the heat. Simmer for 10 minutes. Strain into coffee mugs and serve hot.

HOT SPICED CIDER AND RUM PUNCH

We get many requests at the Cider Mill for punch recipes, both alcoholic and nonalcoholic. This recipe has rum in it and you should not substitute any other liquor for it.

Directions

Prick the oranges with a fork and stud with the cloves. Place in a punch bowl or chafing dish. Heat the cider with the cinnamon sticks in a large saucepan. Pour over the oranges and add the rum. Serve warm in punch cups.

Ingredients

3 small oranges
3 tablespoons whole cloves
8 cups ($^1/_2$ gallon) apple cider
2 cinnamon sticks
$1^1/_2$ cups light or dark rum

Serves Twelve

THE

BRUNCHES

APPLE AND RAISIN MUFFINS

Ingredients

2 cups all-purpose flour
1 cup quick-cooking oats
1/3 cup sugar
1 tablespoon baking powder
1 teaspoon nutmeg
2 teaspoons cinnamon
1 teaspoon salt
1 Ida Red or McIntosh apple, peeled, finely chopped
1 cup golden raisins
1 egg
3/4 cup milk
1/2 cup vegetable oil

Serves Twelve

This muffin variation substitutes the crunch of oats for the crunch of nuts for people who do not care for nuts.

Directions

Preheat the oven to 400 degrees. Line 12 muffin cups with paper cups or spray with nonstick cooking spray. Whisk together the flour, oats, sugar, baking powder, nutmeg, cinnamon and salt in a large bowl. Add the apple and raisins; toss to coat well. Beat the egg in a small bowl. Blend in the milk and oil. Add to the dry ingredients; mix just until moistened. Spoon evenly into the prepared muffin cups. Bake at 400 degrees for 20 to 25 minutes or until the tops are light brown and the edges begin to pull from the sides of the cups.

Ida Red

FRENCH TOAST WITH TOPPING

Ingredients for the French toast

16 (1-inch) slices
good quality dried bread
9 eggs, beaten
2 1/4 cups milk
1 1/2 tablespoons vanilla extract
1 1/2 teaspoons cinnamon
3 tablespoons butter or margarine

Ingredients for the topping

7 tablespoons butter or margarine
1 1/2 pounds Northern Spy or
Granny Smith apples,
peeled, coarsely chopped,
or about 3 medium apples
2/3 cup firmly packed
light brown sugar
1 cup hot water
1 1/2 cups coarsely chopped pecans

Serves Eight

When we welcome weekend guests at our lakeside home, we often start the day with a brunch of fruit, mugs of flavored coffee and French Toast with Topping. It is a change from the standard breakfast of bacon or ham and eggs and is so satisfying that I know I'll have the rest of the day free until it's time to start dinner.

Directions for the French toast

Arrange the bread slices in a single layer in a shallow dish.
Beat the eggs with the milk, vanilla and cinnamon in a bowl.
Pour over the bread. Let stand for 20 minutes or until the egg mixture is absorbed, turning the bread once or twice.
Prepare the topping while the bread is soaking.
Melt 1 tablespoon of the butter in a large heavy skillet over medium heat. Add a single layer of the bread slices.
Cook for about 3 minutes on each side or until golden brown.
Remove to a warm platter.
Repeat the process with the remaining butter and bread slices.
Serve with the apple and pecan topping.

Directions for the topping

Melt the butter in a large heavy saucepan over medium heat.
Add the apples. Sauté for 5 minutes.
Add the brown sugar and hot water.
Cook for 5 minutes or until thickened, stirring constantly.
Stir in the pecans; keep warm.

THE
Midwest Edition
What's
Business and Finance

STREUSEL COFFEE CAKES

Ingredients

2 1/2 cup firmly packed brown sugar
1/2 cup rolled oats
2 teaspoons cinnamon
1/4 cup (1/2 stick) butter or margarine, chilled
3 cups all-purpose flour
1 1/2 teaspoons baking powder
1 1/2 teaspoons baking soda
1/2 teaspoon nutmeg
1/2 teaspoon salt
3/4 cup (1 1/2 sticks) butter or margarine, softened
1 1/3 cups sugar
3 eggs
1 teaspoon vanilla extract
1 1/2 cups plain yogurt
1 cup apple butter

Serves Twenty-Four

There are many recipes for Streusel Coffee Cake. The yogurt and apple butter in this coffee cake, however, make it especially moist and flavorful.

Directions

Preheat the oven to 350 degrees. Grease two 5x9-inch loaf pans. Mix the brown sugar, oats and cinnamon in a bowl. Cut in 1/4 cup chilled butter with a pastry blender or work in with fingers until the mixture resembles coarse meal. Set aside for topping. Sift the flour, baking powder, baking soda, nutmeg and salt together. Cream 3/4 cup butter and sugar in a large mixer bowl until fluffy. Beat in the eggs 1 at a time. Add the vanilla. Fold in the sifted dry ingredients alternately with the yogurt, beginning and ending with the dry ingredients and mixing well after each addition. Spoon about 1 1/2 cups batter into each prepared loaf pan. Sprinkle each with half the streusel topping; spread with the apple butter. Top with the remaining batter and streusel topping. Cut through with a knife to swirl the mixtures. Bake at 350 degrees for 45 minutes or until the top is golden brown and tester comes out clean. Remove to a wire rack. Serve warm or at room temperature.

Rome

Perfectly round and nearly solid red, with the look of a "storybook" apple, the Rome was not named after the ancient city, but rather after Rome Township, Ohio, where it was discovered in 1816. The fruit has a tough, smooth skin and the flesh is sweet with a tinge of yellow and green coloring. Because the fruit is very firm, it has an excellent storage and shelf life with the ability to retain its flavor and shape in baking.

APPLE STRUDEL PASTRIES

Ingredients

1 1/2 cups finely chopped peeled Empire apples, or about 3 medium apples
1/3 cup sugar
3 tablespoons boiled apple cider (page 74)
1/2 teaspoon cinnamon
1/4 cup sliced almonds
1 (17 1/4-ounce) package frozen puff pastry, thawed
1 egg, beaten
2 tablespoons water
Confectioners' sugar

Serves Twelve

Strudel is a type of pastry made up of many layers of very thin dough spread with a filling. My one and only experience in attempting to make strudel dough was such a disaster that my guests ate only the filling and left the pastry. Today we are all too busy to spend the time required to make the pastry, but the frozen puff pastry sheets work very well, and in some cases, better. These pastries are best served the day they are made.

Directions

Preheat the oven to 350 degrees. Combine the apples, sugar, boiled cider and cinnamon in a medium saucepan. Bring to a boil and reduce the heat. Simmer, covered, for 20 minutes or until the apples are tender and the syrup is slightly thickened. Cool to room temperature. Stir in the almonds.

Unfold the pastry sheets and cut each into six 3x5-inch rectangles. Brush with a mixture of egg and water. Place 1 tablespoon of the apple mixture in the center of each pastry rectangle, spreading to within 1/2 inch of edges. Roll the pastry from a long side to enclose the filling, pinching the edges and seams to seal. Brush with the egg mixture.

Place on a lightly greased baking sheet. Bake at 350 degrees for 25 to 30 minutes or until light brown. Cool slightly and sprinkle with confectioners' sugar.

Serve warm or at room temperature.

Empire

SWEET APPLE MUFFINS

We enjoy many variations of muffins. This recipe came from my friend Cathy Tassinari and was originally made with blueberries. I substituted chopped apples for the blueberries and found the muffins to be moist and delicious.

Directions

Preheat the oven to 400 degrees. Line 18 muffin cups with paper liners or spray with nonstick cooking spray. Whisk the flour, sugar, baking powder, cinnamon and salt in a large bowl. Add the apples and pecans; toss to coat well. Beat the eggs with the milk and oil in a small bowl. Add to the dry ingredients, mixing just until moistened. Spoon evenly into the prepared muffin cups, filling 2/3 full. Sprinkle with additional sugar. Bake at 400 degrees for 20 to 25 minutes or until light brown on top and the edges begin to pull from the sides of the muffin cups. Serve warm or at room temperature.

Ingredients

3 cups all-purpose flour
1 cup sugar
4 teaspoons baking powder
1 teaspoon cinnamon
1 teaspoon salt
2 cups finely chopped peeled Empire apples, or about 2 large apples
½ cup chopped pecans (optional)
2 eggs, beaten
1 cup milk
½ cup vegetable oil

Serves Eighteen

APPLE BUTTER NUT BREAD

Ingredients for the bread

2 cups all-purpose flour
1 teaspoon baking powder
1 teaspoon cinnamon
1 1/4 teaspoons nutmeg
1 cup vegetable oil
2 eggs
1 cup sugar
3/4 cup apple butter
1/2 cup golden raisins
1/2 cup chopped pecans

Ingredients for the glaze

2 tablespoons apple cider or apple juice
2 cups sifted confectioners' sugar
1 teaspoon light corn syrup
1/4 teaspoon cinnamon

Serves Sixteen

Apple Butter Nut Bread is so moist that it will keep for several days. It is particularly good in the morning, but it could also be served with a meal or as a sandwich with a whipped cream cheese filling. It will freeze well, but should be glazed just before serving. Apple butter is available at most supermarkets. It keeps well, but must be refrigerated once it is opened. This recipe makes two small loaves.

Directions for the bread

Preheat the oven to 375 degrees. Sift together the flour, baking powder, cinnamon and nutmeg and set aside. Beat the oil, eggs and sugar in large mixer bowl until smooth. Stir in the apple butter, raisins and pecans. Add the dry ingredients, mixing just until moistened. Spoon into 2 greased 3x7-inch loaf pans. Bake at 375 degrees for 45 minutes or until tester comes out clean, covering with foil if necessary to prevent overbrowning. Cool in pans on a wire rack for 10 minutes. Remove to the wire rack to cool completely. Spread with glaze. Store wrapped in foil.

Directions for the glaze

Combine the apple cider, confectioners' sugar, corn syrup and cinnamon in a bowl; mix until smooth.

Paula Red

APPLE NUT BREAD

Ingredients

3 cups all-purpose flour
1 teaspoon baking soda
1 teaspoon salt
1 cup chopped walnuts
3 cups finely chopped peeled Jonathan or McIntosh apples, or about 3 medium apples
1 cup vegetable oil
2 cups sugar
3 eggs, slightly beaten
2 teaspoons cinnamon

Serves Sixteen

Nut bread, always one of my favorites, is delicious for breakfast with a cup of steaming hot coffee or on a brunch menu featuring an egg dish and fresh fruit bowl. This recipe makes two small loaves.

Directions

Preheat the oven to 300 degrees. Mix the flour, baking soda, salt, walnuts and apples in a large bowl. Add the oil, sugar, eggs and cinnamon; mix just until moistened. Spoon into 2 greased and floured 3x7-inch loaf pans. Bake at 300 degrees for 1 1/2 hours or until tester comes out clean. Remove to a wire rack to cool.

McIntosh

Probably one of the most popular and best-tasting varieties grown, the variety originated from a tree that was discovered by John McIntosh on his farm near Dundela, Ontario, in 1796. It is a juicy, aromatic, slightly tart apple with a tough skin, very white flesh and a mixed red and green coloring. Many new varieties have been developed from a McIntosh cross, some to ripen earlier than the parent, and others to suit particular growing conditions. Some of these are the Cortland, Early McIntosh, Empire, Jonamac, Macoun and Spartan. Besides being a delightful eating apple, McIntosh perks up salads, and makes an especially tasty applesauce and apple pie.

SIDE DISHES

CURRIED SQUASH SOUP

Ingredients

1 cup chopped onion
2 tablespoons olive oil or vegetable oil
1 1/2 teaspoons curry powder
2 small (1 1/4-pound) butternut squash, peeled, cut into 1-inch cubes
2 medium Winesap apples, peeled, chopped
1 (14-ounce) can chicken broth
1 1/2 cups water
1 1/4 teaspoons salt
Pepper to taste
1 1/2 cups half-and-half or 1 (12-ounce) can evaporated skim milk

Garnish

Chopped parsley or chives
Sour cream

Serves Four

Curried Squash Soup is rich enough to serve as a main course for a light supper. It is good with a hearty rye bread and a chilled bottle of your favorite white wine. Remember that curry powder must be stored in an airtight container and that it loses its pungency after two months.

Directions

Sauté the onion in heated olive oil in a 4-quart saucepan over medium heat for 15 minutes or until tender. Stir in the curry powder. Cook for 1 minute longer. Add the squash, apples, chicken broth, water, salt and pepper. Bring to a boil and reduce the heat to low. Simmer for 10 to 15 minutes or until the squash is very tender, stirring frequently. Process the mixture in several portions in a food processor until smooth. Combine the portions in a saucepan. Add the half-and-half and mix well. Cook until heated through, stirring occasionally. Garnish the servings with parsley or chives and sour cream.

Winesap

Winesap has long been one of the most popular varieties in America, although newer varieties and changing consumer tastes have claimed some of its market share. Winesaps are medium in size, with a somewhat oblong shape; the skin is deep red with yellow showing. The flesh is yellowish, firm and crisp, with a sweet, aromatic flavor. The variety is good both for cooking and for eating fresh.

APPLESAUCE AND RASPBERRY SALAD

Ingredients

1 (3-ounce) package raspberry gelatin
1 cup boiling water
1 (10-ounce) package frozen raspberries
1 cup applesauce
1 cup sour cream
2 tablespoons sugar
1½ cups miniature marshmallows

Serves Six to Nine

My mother and aunt frequently made gelatin salads for special dinners and our annual Fourth of July picnic. In later years, I realized that they preferred gelatin salads to fresh salads because those salads could be made in advance to avoid last-minute preparations. This is one of those make-ahead salads.

Directions

Dissolve the gelatin in the boiling water in a bowl. Add the frozen raspberries, stirring to dissolve. Stir in the applesauce. Spoon into a 8x8-inch dish or 2-quart mold. Chill until set. Combine the sour cream and sugar in a bowl; stir to dissolve the sugar. Stir in the marshmallows. Spread over the congealed mixture. Cut the salad into squares and serve on lettuce leaves.

APPLE AND CELERY SALAD

Ingredients

½ cup walnuts (optional)
¼ cup mayonnaise
2 tablespoons Cognac or other brandy
3 tablespoons horseradish
2 tablespoons sugar
1 tablespoon lemon juice
⅔ cup whipping cream, chilled
4 stalks celery, coarsely chopped
2 Red Delicious apples, chopped
Salt and pepper to taste

Serves Four

Apple and Celery Salad is easy to prepare and is a nice accompaniment to meat or poultry dishes. Choose the best apples the market has to offer, leaving the skin on for additional color.

Directions

Preheat the oven to 350 degrees. Toast the walnuts in a single layer on a baking sheet at 350 degrees for 10 to 15 minutes or until golden brown. Cool to room temperature. Combine the mayonnaise, brandy, horseradish, sugar and lemon juice in a medium bowl; mix well. Beat the whipping cream in a large mixer bowl until soft peaks form. Fold in the mayonnaise mixture. Add the celery, apples, salt and pepper. Spoon into a serving bowl and sprinkle with the toasted walnuts. Chill until serving time.

DRIED CHERRY CHICKEN SALAD

Ingredients

1 cup dried tart red cherries
4 chicken breast halves, cooked, torn into large pieces
3 stalks celery, coarsely chopped
2 Granny Smith apples, coarsely chopped
1 cup coarsely chopped pecans
1¼ cups mayonnaise
½ cup chopped parsley
1 tablespoon raspberry vinegar
Salt and pepper to taste

Garnish

Dried tart red cherries

Serves Six

Dried Cherry Chicken Salad was a favorite recipe at our daughter Julie's gourmet shop. Serve it as the star attraction at a luncheon with just a muffin and a beverage to complete the meal. Dried tart red cherries are available at specialty food shops.

Directions

Mix the 1 cup cherries, chicken, celery, apples and pecans in a large bowl. Combine the mayonnaise, parsley and raspberry vinegar in a bowl; mix well. Add to the chicken mixture and toss lightly to coat well. Season with salt and pepper. Chill for 2 hours or longer. Serve on a bed of red leaf lettuce. Garnish with additional cherries.

Cortland

Cortlands were first raised in 1898 at the New York State Agricultural Experiment Station from a cross between Ben Davis and McIntosh varieties. It is a dessert-type apple that has found acceptance for eating fresh. Cortland is a very "natural" looking apple, with a base color of pale yellow almost completely flushed with a deep red or crimson and highlighted by very short dark red stripes and grey green dots. The Cortland variety has a very white flesh with a slightly tinged green color near the core. It is slightly coarse-textured, moderately juicy, with a sweet refreshing flavor.

BAKED APPLESAUCE

Ingredients

6 medium Northern Spy apples, peeled, sliced, or about 2 pounds
½ cup sugar
¼ cup water
1 teaspoon cinnamon

Serves Twelve

Baked applesauce does not need as much watching as applesauce prepared on top of the stove. It is a nice accompaniment to roast pork and could bake along with the roast. It is especially good served warm.

Directions

Preheat the oven to 350 degrees. Combine the apples, sugar and water in a 2-quart baking dish; mix well. Bake, covered, at 350 degrees for 30 to 40 minutes or until the apples are tender and can be mashed with a fork. Stir in the cinnamon. Serve warm or at room temperature.

Northern Spy

The Northern Spy, an old favorite and a popular cooking apple, is harvested late in the fall, as it is one of the last to ripen. It has a yellow-green skin with a red blush and a yellowish flesh which holds its shape and flavor in cooking. It was discovered near Rochester, New York, around 1800, and is believed to be a descendant of the Wagener.

RED CABBAGE AND APPLES

Red Cabbage and Apples is a dressed-up cabbage dish that can be prepared in advance and reheated at serving time. It especially complements a roasted pork loin. Add your favorite green vegetable and hot rolls to complete the meal.

Directions

Cook the bacon and onion in a 4-quart saucepan until the bacon is crisp and the onion is light brown. Stir in the cabbage, apples, salt and pepper. Add the wine and hot water. Simmer, covered, for 1 hour, stirring occasionally. Serve hot.

Ingredients

4 ounces bacon, cut into 1/2-inch pieces
1/2 cup chopped onion
1 medium red cabbage, shredded
2 Rome Beauty apples, peeled, coarsely chopped
Salt and pepper to taste
3/4 cup dry white wine
3/4 cup hot water

Serves Six

SWEET POTATOES AND APPLES

Ingredients

3 very large orange-fleshed sweet potatoes, or about 3 pounds
1 3/4 pounds Jonathan apples
1/4 cup apple cider
1 cup maple syrup
1/4 cup (1/2 stick) butter or margarine, cut into pieces
1 teaspoon cinnamon
1/2 teaspoon salt

Serves Six to Eight

The combination of apples and sweet potatoes is very compatible. This combination dish can be served with poultry or ham and would be a nice change from the candied sweet potatoes so often served at Thanksgiving.

Directions

Preheat the oven to 375 degrees. Peel the sweet potatoes and cut them crosswise into 1/4-inch slices. Peel and core the apples and cut into 1/4-inch slices. Alternate the apple slices and sweet potato slices in a circle in a baking dish, filling the center with remaining slices. Combine the apple cider, maple syrup, butter, cinnamon and salt in a medium saucepan. Bring to a boil over high heat. Pour over the sweet potatoes and apples. Bake, tightly covered, at 375 degrees, for 1 hour. Reduce the oven temperature to 350 degrees. Bake, uncovered, for 15 minutes longer or until the sweet potatoes and apples are tender and the syrup is reduced to a thick glaze, basting occasionally. Serve immediately.

Jonagold

Jonagold originated at the Agriculture Research Station in Geneva, New York, from a cross of Golden Delicious and Jonathan. Jonagold is best grown in Michigan because it demands a cooler climate. It has an orange-red blush over a yellow background. It is a firm and juicy all-purpose apple with an excellent flavor characteristic to its parentage.

APPLE CHUTNEY

Ingredients

3 Winesap apples, peeled, coarsely chopped
1/2 cup golden raisins
1 cup firmly packed brown sugar
3/4 cup cider vinegar
2 ounces fresh ginger, finely chopped
1 clove of garlic, finely chopped
1 teaspoon salt

Yields One Pint

My cousin Gertrude makes this chutney using mangoes for the fruit. I substituted apples for the mangoes and we think it is delicious. Try serving it with pork or as an appetizer with crackers and a soft creamy cheese such as Brie.

Directions

Combine the apples, raisins, brown sugar, vinegar, ginger, garlic and salt in a medium saucepan; mix well. Bring to a boil and reduce the heat. Simmer for 45 to 50 minutes or until of the desired consistency.

APPLE CIDER VINAIGRETTE

Ingredients

1/2 cup safflower oil
3 tablespoons apple cider vinegar
2 tablespoons fresh lemon juice
1 tablespoon sugar
Paprika, salt and pepper to taste

Serves Six

Apple Cider Vinaigrette, made with just the correct proportions of oil to vinegar, can make an ordinary salad great. Try it with a mixed green salad or pasta salad.

Directions

Combine the oil, vinegar, lemon juice, sugar, paprika, salt and pepper in a covered jar. Shake to mix well. Serve over fresh greens or pasta salad.

MAIN DISHES

APPLE AND SAUSAGE RING

Ingredients

1 Jonathan apple, peeled, finely chopped
2 pounds mild pork sausage
2 eggs, slightly beaten
1/2 cup milk
1 1/2 cups herb stuffing mix
1/4 cup minced onion

Garnish

Apple slices

Serves Six to Eight

Apple and Sausage Ring is a change from a ground beef meat loaf. The flavor is unusual and the preparation time minimal. Leftovers make an excellent sandwich, especially on sourdough bread.

Directions

Preheat the oven to 350 degrees. Combine the apple, sausage, eggs, milk, stuffing mix and onion in a large bowl; mix well. Press into a 10-inch ring mold. Bake at 350 degrees for 1 hour or until cooked through; drain well. Invert onto a serving platter. Garnish with apple slices and serve immediately.

Jonathan

COMPANY PORK CHOPS

Ingredients

6 Ida Red apples, peeled, thickly sliced
6 pork chops
2 teaspoons butter or margarine
6 tablespoons brown sugar
6 tablespoons catsup

Serves Six

Company Pork Chops is a recipe from a friend. It is a treat and special enough, as the name implies, for entertaining. Serve it with a rice medley and a green vegetable.

Directions

Preheat the oven to 375 degrees. Line a large baking dish with enough foil to overlap the casserole and seal. Arrange the apple slices in a single layer in the prepared dish. Brown the pork chops in the butter in a skillet. Arrange over the apples. Sprinkle with the brown sugar and spread with the catsup. Fold the foil over the pork chops, sealing with a double fold. Bake at 375 degrees for 1 hour or until the pork chops and apples are tender. Serve immediately.

Ida Red

This bright red apple is being grown extensively because of its excellent keeping ability and its growing popularity as a pie apple. Developed in Moscow, Idaho, at the Idaho Experiment Station, it was introduced commercially in 1942, and is a cross between a Jonathan and a Wagener. Ida Red has firm, crisp and juicy flesh bursting with Jonathan-like flavor. For those who like a tart and tangy flavor, the Ida Red is a favorite. It is also excellent for baking, sauces, and pies.

SAUSAGE AND SAUERKRAUT BAKE

Ingredients

1 pound mild Italian sausage
1 cup chopped onion
2 Ida Red apples,
peeled, cut into quarters
1 (27-ounce) can
sauerkraut, drained
1 cup dry white wine
2 tablespoons firmly packed
brown sugar
2 teaspoons caraway seeds
1 teaspoon salt
1/2 teaspoon pepper

Garnish

Parsley

Serves Six

This is a wonderful casserole to pop in the oven when I arrive home from a busy day at the Cider Mill. Serve it with warm corn bread sticks and parslied buttered carrots for a hearty fall meal.

Directions

Preheat the oven to 350 degrees. Cut the sausage into 1-inch slices. Brown with the onion in a large skillet, stirring until the sausage is crumbly and the onion is tender; drain. Stir in the apples, sauerkraut, wine, brown sugar, caraway seeds, salt and pepper. Spoon into a 2 1/2-quart baking dish. Bake, covered, at 350 degrees for 1 hour. Garnish with parsley.

Northern Spy

CURRIED CHICKEN BAKE

Ingredients

3 Empire apples, peeled, thickly sliced
1 tablespoon butter or margarine
1 tablespoon sugar
4 chicken breast halves
1/2 cup mayonnaise
1/2 teaspoon soy sauce
1/2 teaspoon Dijon mustard
1/2 teaspoon prepared horseradish
2 teaspoons curry powder

Serves Four

Casseroles that can be made ahead and baked at the last minute after work or play are especially welcome. Curried Chicken Bake is easy enough for a casual, relaxed supper and special enough to serve to company.

Directions

Preheat the oven to 350 degrees. Sauté the apples in the butter in a skillet over low heat for 5 to 7 minutes. Add the sugar and increase the heat to medium. Sauté until the apples are brown. Spread in a greased 9x13-inch baking dish. Rinse the chicken in cold water and pat dry. Combine the mayonnaise, soy sauce, mustard, horseradish and curry powder in a bowl; mix well. Spread over both sides of the chicken. Arrange chicken skin side up over the apples. Bake at 350 degrees for 1 hour or until chicken is cooked through. You may chill the dish for up to 24 hours before baking or double the recipe if desired.

Empire

Developed by Dr. Roger Way at the Geneva Agricultural Experiment Station at Cornell University, the Empire apple is fast growing in popularity. Named in 1966, it is a cross between a McIntosh and a Red Delicious and takes on the best characteristics of the two popular varieties. It is excellent for fresh eating and is also a high-quality dessert apple. Empires are excellent when used for salads, baking and cooking. The apple is widely grown in New York, Ontario and Michigan, with a large percentage of the crop being shipped to the United Kingdom.

CIDER-MARINATED LAMB CHOPS

Ingredients

1/2 cup apple cider
1/4 cup firmly packed brown sugar
1 teaspoon dry mustard
1/4 teaspoon ground cloves
1/2 teaspoon garlic salt
4 (6-ounce) sirloin lamb chops or lean rib lamb chops

Serves Four

The cider mellows the flavor of the lamb in Cider-Marinated Lamb Chops, which can be prepared on the grill or in the broiler. Serve the chops with fettuccini, buttered asparagus and mint jelly.

Directions

Combine the apple cider, brown sugar, dry mustard, cloves and garlic salt in a large sealable plastic bag. Trim the fat from the lamb chops and add to the marinade; seal the bag. Marinate in the refrigerator for 2 hours or longer, turning the bag occasionally. Drain, reserving the marinade. Preheat the grill or broiler. Grill the lamb chops for 6 minutes on each side or broil 5 inches from heat source for 9 minutes on each side or until done to taste, basting frequently with the reserved marinade.

Golden Delicious

The Golden Delicious is a sunshine yellow apple with a thin skin and a sweet and juicy flesh. It has an excellent eating flavor as well as a distinctive aromatic flavor that is actually enhanced by cooking. It is a good apple to use in recipes in which the apple pieces need to hold their shape. Golden Delicious makes a good choice for apple cakes and pies, baked apples, applesauce and salads, because very little sugar needs to be added. Although similar to a Red Delicious in name and flavor, it is not genetically related. It was discovered in West Virginia in 1890 and is thought to have grown from a seed which was a cross between a Golden Reinette and a Grimes Golden.

DESSERTS

BUTTERMILK APPLE CAKE

Ingredients

4 cups all-purpose flour
2 teaspoons baking soda
2 teaspoons cinnamon
1 teaspoon allspice
1 teaspoon cloves
1 teaspoon nutmeg
1 cup (2 sticks) butter or margarine, softened
2 cups sugar
2 cups buttermilk
1 cup chopped walnuts or pecans
2 cups golden raisins
1 Gala or McIntosh apple, peeled, finely chopped

Serves Twelve

The recipe for Buttermilk Apple Cake was given to me many years ago by my college roommate's mother. The addition of chopped apple makes it even better than the original recipe. The large cake, made in a 10-inch bundt or tube pan, doesn't require frosting and keeps very well.

Directions

Preheat the oven to 350 degrees. Mix the flour, baking soda, cinnamon, allspice, cloves and nutmeg together and set aside. Cream the butter and sugar in a large mixer bowl until light and fluffy. Beat in 1/4 of the flour mixture. Add the buttermilk and remaining flour mixture 1/3 at a time, ending with the flour mixture and mixing constantly at medium speed and scraping down the side of the bowl. Add the walnuts, raisins and apple; mix for 30 seconds longer. Spoon into a 10-inch bundt or tube pan sprayed with nonstick cooking spray. Bake at 350 degrees for 1 hour and 10 minutes or until tester comes out clean. Cool in the pan for 10 minutes. Remove to a wire rack to cool completely.

Gala

The Gala was developed in 1939, as a cross between a Kidds Orange and a Golden Delicious. Gala had its origin in New Zealand and was released in 1960 by J.H. Kidd of Greytown. It was brought to the U.S. in 1972 by Stark Brother's Nursery. Color patterns range from a striped orange and yellow to a full red orange. Gala's outstanding feature is its excellent eating quality. It has a very firm yellow flesh with a sweet flavor.

APPLE BUTTER CAKES

Ingredients

3/4 cup (1 1/2 sticks) butter or margarine, softened
1 1/4 cups firmly packed brown sugar
3 eggs
1 teaspoon vanilla extract
2 1/4 cups all-purpose flour
2 teaspoons baking soda
2 1/4 teaspoons apple pie spice
1/2 teaspoon salt
1 1/2 cups apple butter
1/3 cup skim milk
1 cup golden raisins
1 cup chopped pecans or walnuts
Boiled Cider Rum Sauce (page 67)

Serves Twelve

The Apple Butter Cakes recipe makes two layers. If you do not need both layers at one time, you can freeze the extra layer. Serve it with the Boiled Cider Rum Sauce on page 67, which is so pungent that you can pour a small amount over each serving and pass the extra for guests to add if they wish.

Directions

Preheat the oven to 350 degrees. Cream the butter and brown sugar in a mixer bowl until light and fluffy. Beat in the eggs and vanilla. Mix the flour, baking soda, apple pie spice and salt together. Mix the apple butter with the milk in a small bowl. Add the flour mixture to the creamed mixture in thirds alternately with the apple butter mixture, beginning and ending with the flour and mixing well after each addition.
Fold in the raisins and pecans gently. Spoon into 2 greased and floured 9-inch cake pans. Bake at 350 degrees for 25 to 30 minutes or until tester comes out clean. Cool in pans for 15 minutes. Remove to a wire rack to cool completely.
Cut the layers into wedges and serve with vanilla ice cream and Boiled Cider Rum Sauce.

Cortland

BOILED CIDER RUM SAUCE

Boiled Cider Rum Sauce is also delicious over butter-pecan ice cream or French toast.

Directions

Whisk the rum, brown sugar, cornstarch, Boiled Cider, cinnamon, nutmeg and salt in a medium saucepan. Bring to a boil over medium heat. Add the butter. Boil for 2 minutes; remove from the heat. Keep warm until ready to serve or chill until serving time and reheat to serve.

Ingredients

1/2 cup dark rum
1/4 cup firmly packed brown sugar
1 1/2 tablespoons cornstarch
1 1/4 cups boiled cider (page 74)
1/4 teaspoon cinnamon
Nutmeg and salt to taste
2 tablespoons butter or margarine

Yields Two Cups

GRATED APPLE CAKE

Ingredients

1/2 cup (1 stick) butter or margarine, softened
2/3 cup sugar
1/2 cup firmly packed dark brown sugar
2 eggs
1 teaspoon lemon juice
1 teaspoon grated lemon rind
2 1/3 cups all-purpose flour
1 teaspoon baking powder
1 teaspoon baking soda
1/2 teaspoon nutmeg
1 teaspoon cinnamon
1 teaspoon allspice
1 cup chopped walnuts
2 1/3 cups finely chopped peeled Northern Spy or Jonathan apples
2/3 cup chopped walnuts
1 tablespoon sugar
1 teaspoon cinnamon

Serves Twelve

Grated Apple Cake is good enough to be served plain with just the topping included here. It can also be served with ice cream or with a buttercream frosting.

Directions

Preheat the oven to 350 degrees. Cream the butter, 2/3 cup sugar and brown sugar in a mixer bowl until light and fluffy. Beat in the eggs 1 at a time. Add the lemon juice and lemon rind; mix well. Sift the flour, baking powder, baking soda, nutmeg, 1 teaspoon cinnamon and allspice together. Add to the creamed mixture; mix well. Fold in 1 cup walnuts and apples. Spoon into a 9-inch tube pan sprayed with nonstick cooking spray. Combine 2/3 cup walnuts, 1 tablespoon sugar and 1 teaspoon cinnamon in a small bowl; mix well. Spread over the batter. Bake at 350 degrees for 40 minutes or until cake tester comes out clean. Cool in pan for 10 minutes. Invert onto a wire rack to cool completely.

Jonathan

The Jonathan was discovered in 1826 in Woodstock, New York. It is a versatile all-purpose crimson apple with a sweet, some say, spicy flavor. It is still widely grown, although newer varieties adapt better to modern storage. It is excellent for pies and sauces and superior for baking, salads, and eating out-of-hand.

APPLE AND RHUBARB PIE

Ingredients for the filling

2 cups thinly sliced
Granny Smith apples,
or 2 medium apples
3 cups (1-inch) pieces of rhubarb
1½ cups sugar
1 tablespoon tapioca
1 teaspoon cinnamon

Ingredients for the pastry

3 cups all-purpose flour
1 teaspoon salt
1 cup plus 2 tablespoons
vegetable shortening
½ cup (or more) ice water
1 tablespoon butter or margarine

Serves Eight

Most of us think of baking with apples in the fall when the supply is plentiful. About the first of May, however, fresh rhubarb becomes available and it pairs perfectly with apples for a spring pie. This recipe makes a generous 9-inch pie. A tip I learned from my mother-in-law, who bakes our pies at the Cider Mill, is to not blend the shortening too much into the flour mixture. For a flaky pastry, she blends in the shortening only until the mixture resembles large peas.

Directions to make the filling

Combine the apples, rhubarb, sugar, tapioca and cinnamon in a large bowl; mix lightly.

Directions to make the pastry and bake the pie

Preheat the oven to 400 degrees. Mix the flour and salt in a bowl. Cut in the shortening with a pastry blender until the mixture resembles large peas. Add the ice water and mix with a fork to form dough. Divide the pastry into 2 portions. Roll 1 portion to fit a 9-inch pie plate and fit it into the plate. Spoon the filling into the prepared pie plate. Dot with the butter. Roll the remaining pastry and fit it over the pie. Trim and seal the edge and cut vents. Bake at 400 degrees for 15 minutes. Reduce the oven temperature to 375 degrees. Bake the pie for 45 minutes longer or until the crust is golden brown.

Golden Delicious

CRAN-APPLE PIE

Ingredients for the pastry

1 cup all-purpose flour
2 tablespoons sugar
1/2 teaspoon salt
1/2 cup (1 stick) butter, chilled, cut into small pieces
2 to 3 tablespoons ice water

Ingredients for the filling

4 to 5 Northern Spy apples, peeled, coarsely chopped
1/4 cup fresh or frozen cranberries
1/2 cup sugar
2 tablespoons boiled cider (page 74)
Salt to taste

Ingredients for the topping

1/4 cup (1/2 stick) butter, chilled, cut into small pieces
1/2 cup all-purpose flour
1/3 cup firmly packed brown sugar

Serves Six to Eight

The combination of cranberries and apples in this recipe is a satisfying taste experience.

Directions to make the pastry

Mix the flour, sugar and salt in a medium bowl. Cut in the butter until the mixture resembles large peas. Add enough water to form dough, mixing with a fork. Roll into a ball. Chill, wrapped in plastic wrap, for 30 minutes. Roll on a lightly floured surface. Fit into a 9-inch pie plate. Trim and flute the edge.

Directions to make the filling

Combine the apples, cranberries, sugar, boiled cider and salt in a bowl; mix gently. Spoon into the prepared pastry.

Directions to make the topping

Combine the butter and flour in a bowl and mix using your fingers until smooth. Add the brown sugar and mix just until moistened; the mixture will be lumpy. Sprinkle the topping over the pie.

To bake and serve the pie

Preheat the oven to 375 degrees. Bake the pie for 45 to 50 minutes or until the pastry is golden brown and the apples are tender. Serve at room temperature with Boiled Cider Rum Sauce (page 67).

Cranberries are grown in huge, sandy bogs on low, trailing vines. They're also called bounceberries, because ripe ones bounce. The cranberry is named after the shape of the shrub's pale pink blossoms, which resemble the heads of the cranes often seen wading through the cranberry bogs. Traditional in cranberry sauce, this fruit also makes a delicious addition to apple pie.

APPLE PIE

Ingredients

8 medium McIntosh or
Granny Smith apples,
peeled, thinly sliced, or 8 cups
2 tablespoons dark rum
1/4 cup boiled apple cider
1 recipe (2-crust) pie pastry
1/2 cup sugar
1/4 cup firmly packed brown sugar
2 tablespoons all-purpose flour
1/4 teaspoon nutmeg
1 tablespoon butter or margarine
Boiled Cider Rum Sauce (page 67)

Serves Six to Eight

This apple pie is good enough to stand alone but served with Boiled Cider Rum Sauce, it becomes a special occasion dessert.

Directions

Preheat the oven to 375 degrees. Combine the apples, rum and boiled cider in a 4-quart saucepan. Bring to a boil over medium-high heat and reduce the heat. Simmer for 15 minutes or just until the apples are tender when pierced with a fork. Spoon into a pastry-lined 9-inch pie plate. Mix the sugar, brown sugar, flour and nutmeg in a small bowl. Sprinkle over the apples; dot with the butter. Top with the remaining pastry; trim and flute the edge and cut vents. Bake the pie at 375 degrees for 1 hour or until the filling is bubbly and the crust is golden brown. Serve with the hot Boiled Cider Rum Sauce spooned over each slice.

Boiled apple cider is a traditional New England syrup made by evaporating fresh apple cider without adding any sugar. This pungent and aromatic syrup adds concentrated flavor to both desserts and savory dishes, and it is used in several recipes in this book. It is also good to use in a marinade for barbecued spareribs or to glaze a pork roast or baked ham.

You may order bottled boiled cider by writing to
Willis and Tina Wood
RD 2
Springfield, Vermont 05156

To prepare your own boiled apple cider at home, boil 3 cups apple cider in a medium saucepan for 20 to 25 minutes or until it is reduced to 1 1/2 cups. Store in a sterilized jar in the refrigerator until needed.

GLAZED FRESH APPLE COOKIES

Ingredients

2 cups all-purpose flour
1 teaspoon baking soda
1/2 cup (1 stick) butter or margarine, softened
1 1/3 cups firmly packed brown sugar
1/2 teaspoon cinnamon
1 teaspoon ground cloves
1/2 teaspoon nutmeg
1/2 teaspoon salt
1 egg
1 medium Jonathan or McIntosh apple, peeled, finely chopped, or 1 cup
1 cup raisins
1 cup chopped walnuts
1/4 cup apple cider or milk
2 cups confectioners' sugar
3 tablespoons apple cider or milk

Yields Four Dozen

If you like a soft cookie, assertively flavored with fresh apples and the addition of apple cider, you will love Glazed Fresh Apple Cookies. Store them in an airtight container as soon as they are cool.

Directions

Preheat the oven to 400 degrees. Sift the flour and baking soda together and set aside. Cream the butter, brown sugar, cinnamon, cloves, nutmeg, salt and egg in a large mixer bowl until light. Add half the flour mixture; mix well. Stir in the apple, raisins and walnuts. Add 1/4 cup apple cider and the remaining flour mixture; mix well. Drop by teaspoonfuls onto a greased cookie sheet. Bake at 400 degrees for 10 minutes. Remove to a wire rack to cool. Blend the confectioners' sugar and 3 tablespoons apple cider in a bowl. Spread over the cookies.

Paula Red

The Paula Red, discovered on the Lewis Arends orchard near Sparta, Michigan, was named after Mr. Arends' wife, Pauline. Paula Red is a short-season apple harvested from late August through late September and is one of the first varieties to reach the market. This good all-purpose apple has a pleasingly tart flavor and light flesh good for eating fresh and cooking. The skin has a yellow-green background with a good solid-red blush much like a McIntosh.

FUDGE BARS

Ingredients

2 (1-ounce) squares unsweetened chocolate
1/2 cup (1 stick) butter or margarine
2/3 cup sweetened applesauce
2 eggs, beaten
1 cup firmly packed brown sugar
1 teaspoon vanilla extract
1 cup sifted all-purpose flour
1/2 teaspoon baking powder
1/2 teaspoon baking soda
1/4 teaspoon salt
3/4 cup chopped walnuts

Yields One Dozen

You may not often think of the combination of chocolate and apples, but Fudge Bars successfully combine the flavors to produce a moist and tasty treat. Try them with tart lemonade for a cooling contrast of flavors.

Directions

Preheat the oven to 350 degrees. Melt the chocolate with the butter in a double boiler over hot water, stirring to blend well; set aside. Combine the applesauce, eggs, brown sugar and vanilla in a large bowl and mix well. Stir in the flour, baking powder, baking soda and salt. Add 1/2 cup of the walnuts and melted chocolate mixture; mix well. Spoon into a greased 8x8-inch baking pan. Sprinkle with the remaining 1/4 cup walnuts. Bake at 350 degrees for 30 minutes. Cool on a wire rack. Cut into 2x2-inch bars.

Spartan

The Spartan is a McIntosh-type apple of Canadian origin. It is a cross between McIntosh and Yellow Newtown Pippen, and looks much like a McIntosh, though it has a firmer and crisper flesh. The Spartan apple variety flavor is fairly rich, sweet and juicy, and is very aromatic even before being cut. Like the McIntosh, it is an excellent apple for eating fresh, as well as for pies, cider and sauces.

GLAZED APPLESAUCE DROP COOKIES

Glazed Applesauce Drop Cookies will take you back to the days when your grandmother always had a full cookie jar, ready for when you dropped by.

Directions to make the cookies

Preheat the oven to 375 degrees. Combine the applesauce, brown sugar, butter and egg in a bowl and mix well. Stir in the flour, baking soda, salt and pecans. Chill, covered, for 1 to 24 hours. Drop the batter by rounded tablespoonfuls 2 inches apart onto an ungreased cookie sheet. Bake at 375 degrees for 10 to 12 minutes or until golden brown. Remove to a wire rack to cool.

Directions to make the cider glaze

Combine the confectioners' sugar, butter, apple cider and vanilla in a bowl; mix until smooth. Spread over the cookies.

Ingredients for the cookies

1/2 cup unsweetened applesauce
1 cup firmly packed brown sugar
1/2 cup (1 stick) butter or margarine, softened
1 egg
1 3/4 cups all-purpose flour
1/2 teaspoon baking soda
1/2 teaspoon salt
3/4 cup chopped pecans (optional)

Ingredients for the cider glaze

1 cup confectioners' sugar
1 tablespoon butter or margarine, softened
1 1/2 tablespoons apple cider or apple juice
1/2 teaspoon vanilla extract

Yields Three and One-half Dozen

APPLE-TOPPED CHEESECAKE

Ingredients

4 medium Golden or Red Delicious apples, peeled, thinly sliced, or 4 cups
5 tablespoons light butter or margarine, softened
1 tablespoon vegetable shortening
1/3 cup sugar
1 cup all-purpose flour
Salt to taste
16 ounces light cream cheese, softened
1/2 cup sugar
1/2 teaspoon vanilla extract
1 (4-ounce) container egg substitute
1/3 cup sugar
1 teaspoon cinnamon
1/4 cup sliced almonds

Serves Twelve

Apple-Topped Cheesecake is one that cheesecake lovers can enjoy without feeling too guilty due to the use of light cream cheese and egg substitute.

Directions

Preheat the oven to 350 degrees. Arrange the apple slices in a single layer in a shallow baking pan. Bake, covered with foil, at 350 degrees for 15 minutes. Cream the butter, shortening and 1/3 cup sugar at medium speed in a large mixer bowl until light and fluffy. Add the flour and salt and mix until crumbly. Pat over the bottom of a 9-inch springform pan. Combine the cream cheese, 1/2 cup sugar and vanilla in a large mixer bowl and beat until smooth. Add the egg substitute and mix well. Spoon into the prepared springform pan. Arrange the warm apples in a circular design over the top. Mix 1/3 cup sugar and cinnamon in a small bowl. Sprinkle the cinnamon-sugar mixture and almonds over the apples. Bake at 350 degrees for 40 minutes or until golden brown. Cool on a wire rack. Place on a serving plate and remove the side of the pan. Chill, covered, for 4 to 24 hours before serving.

Red Delicious

Discovered as a seedling by Jesse Hiatt in an orchard in Peru, Iowa, in 1870 and named by a nurseryman in Missouri in the 1890s, the Red Delicious has revolutionized the domestic apple industry. The flavor of this glossy, red apple with the distinctive five-pointed elongated shape makes it an ideal choice for a snack, salad or dessert fruit. It has a smooth, bright crimson skin and a juicy and crunchy texture that makes it a popular favorite, best when eaten raw.

SERBIAN APPLE PITA

Ingredients for the pastry

1 cup (2 sticks) unsalted butter, softened
2 3/4 cups all-purpose flour
3 tablespoons sugar
3 egg yolks
3 tablespoons sour cream

Ingredients for the filling

3/4 cup sugar
1/2 teaspoon cinnamon
1/2 teaspoon nutmeg
12 cups thinly sliced peeled Jonathan or Northern Spy apples, or about 4 pounds
1/2 cup finely chopped walnuts

Serves Twelve

Serbian Apple Pita is a recipe from a friend whose grandmother had handed it down to her. It is not a Middle Eastern bread, as we think of pita, but a moist and mildly spiced dessert. Glaze it with a mixture of confectioners' sugar and enough apple cider or light cream to make of spreading consistency or sprinkle it with confectioners' sugar.

Directions to make the pastry

Combine the butter and flour in a bowl; mix using your fingers. Add the sugar, egg yolks and sour cream and mix to form a stiff dough. Divide into 2 portions. Roll 1 portion on a lightly floured surface to fit a 9x13-inch baking pan. Roll the remaining pastry to fit the top.

Directions to make the filling and bake the dessert

Preheat the oven to 350 degrees. Mix the sugar, cinnamon and nutmeg in a bowl. Add the apples, tossing lightly to coat. Spoon into the pastry-lined pan. Top with the remaining pastry, sealing and fluting the edges. Prick the top with a fork and sprinkle with the walnuts. Bake at 350 degrees for 45 minutes. Cool on a wire rack. Cut into squares to serve.

Rome

OLD-FASHIONED APPLE FLAN

Ingredients for the filling

1/2 cup raisins
3 tablespoons light or dark rum
6 tablespoons butter
6 McIntosh apples, peeled, thinly sliced, or about 2 pounds
3/4 cup sugar
1 teaspoon vanilla extract

Ingredients for the pastry

2 1/2 cups all-purpose flour
1 teaspoon sugar
1 teaspoon salt
1 cup (2 sticks) butter or margarine, chilled, cut into small pieces
3/4 to 1/2 cup ice water

Serves Six to Eight

A flan is a round pastry tart that can have a sweet filling, such as custard or fruit, or a savory filling of vegetables or meat. Old-Fashioned Apple Flan is baked in a special flan ring, a bottomless metal ring with straight sides. The ring should be placed on a baking sheet to bake.

Directions to make the filling

Soak the raisins in the rum in a small bowl for 15 minutes. Melt the butter in a skillet and heat until light brown. Add the apples, sugar and vanilla. Cook for several minutes. Add the undrained raisins. Cook over medium heat for 10 minutes or until the apples are lightly caramelized, stirring constantly. Cool to room temperature.

Directions to make the pastry and bake the flan

Mix the flour, sugar and salt in a bowl. Cut in the butter until the mixture resembles small peas. Add enough ice water to form a dough. Chill for 30 minutes. Preheat the oven to 400 degrees. Divide the dough into 1/3 and 2/3 portions. Roll the large portion between 2 sheets of waxed paper to fit a 9-inch flan pan; trim the edge. Place the flan pan on a baking sheet. Fill with the apple mixture. Roll the small pastry portion between 2 sheets of waxed paper and cut into strips. Arrange in a lattice over the apples. Bake at 400 degrees for 40 minutes or until the crust is golden brown. Remove to a wire rack to cool. Serve warm or at room temperature with a scoop of vanilla ice cream if desired.

SOUR CREAM APPLE SQUARES

Ingredients

2 cups all-purpose flour
2 cups firmly packed brown sugar
1/2 cup (1 stick) butter or margarine, softened
1 cup chopped walnuts or pecans
1 cup sour cream
1 egg
1 teaspoon baking soda
2 teaspoons cinnamon
1/2 teaspoon salt
1 teaspoon vanilla extract
2 medium Ida Red apples, peeled, finely chopped, or 2 cups

Serves Twelve to Fifteen

Sour Cream Apple Squares are amazingly easy to prepare, especially for last-minute company, since they are best served the day they are made. Top them off with whipped cream or ice cream.

Directions

Preheat the oven to 350 degrees. Mix the flour and brown sugar in a mixer bowl. Blend in the butter at low speed until the mixture is crumbly. Stir in the walnuts. Press 2 3/4 cups of the mixture into a greased 9x13-inch baking pan. Add the sour cream, egg, baking soda, cinnamon, salt and vanilla to the remaining crumb mixture; mix well. Stir in the apples. Spread evenly in the prepared pan. Bake at 350 degrees for 25 to 35 minutes or until a tester inserted in the center comes out clean. Cut into squares to serve.

Ginger Gold

Ginger Gold was discovered as a chance seedling in an orchard in Virginia. It is similar to the Golden Delicious in appearance and taste, but becomes ready for harvest about six weeks earlier. It exhibits all of the excellent qualities of a Golden Delicious, with a similar texture and sweetness, but a mildly spicy flavor that makes it unique.

APPLE BARS

Apple Bars are perfect for a tailgate picnic, especially in the fall, when apples are so plentiful and have such wonderful flavor.

Directions

Preheat the oven to 350 degrees. Sift the flour, baking powder, cinnamon and salt together. Combine the butter, sugar, brown sugar, eggs and vanilla in a large mixer bowl and mix until smooth. Stir in the sifted dry ingredients, apple, raisins and pecans. Spread in a 9x13-inch baking pan sprayed with nonstick cooking spray. Bake at 350 degrees for 30 to 35 minutes or until the edges pull from the sides of the pan. Cool on a wire rack. Mix the confectioners' sugar and apple cider in a bowl. Spread over the cooled layer. Cut into bars.

Ingredients

2 cups all-purpose flour
2 teaspoons baking powder
1/2 teaspoon cinnamon
1/2 teaspoon salt
1/2 cup melted butter or margarine
1 cup sugar
1 cup firmly packed brown sugar
2 eggs
2 teaspoons vanilla extract
1 medium McIntosh apple, peeled, finely chopped, or 1 cup
1 cup raisins
1 cup coarsely chopped pecans
2 cups confectioners' sugar
1/4 cup apple cider

Yields Two Dozen

BUTTERY APPLE SQUARES

Ingredients for the apple squares

2 cups all-purpose flour
1 teaspoon salt
2/3 cup butter or margarine, chilled
1 egg yolk
1/2 cup milk
5 medium Rome Beauty apples, peeled, thinly sliced, or 5 cups
2 tablespoons flour
3/4 cup sugar
1 teaspoon cinnamon
1 tablespoon butter or margarine
1 egg white, slightly beaten

Ingredients for the frosting

1/2 cup confectioners' sugar
2 tablespoons light cream or milk
1/2 teaspoon vanilla extract

Serves Ten

Buttery Apple Squares are great lunch box or picnic treats.

Directions to make the apple squares

Preheat the oven to 375 degrees. Sift 2 cups flour and salt into a bowl. Cut in 2/3 cup butter until the mixture resembles large peas. Add a mixture of the egg yolk and milk, mixing just until moistened. Divide the dough into 2 equal portions and pat 1 of the portions over the bottom of a greased 7x10-inch baking pan. Spread the apples in the prepared pan. Mix 2 tablespoons flour, sugar and cinnamon in a small bowl. Sprinkle over the apples and dot with 1 tablespoon butter. Roll the remaining dough on a lightly floured surface. Place it over the apples; seal the edges and cut vents. Brush lightly with the egg white. Bake at 375 degrees for 1 hour or until the crust is light brown and the apples are tender.

Directions to make the frosting

Combine the confectioners' sugar, cream and vanilla in a bowl and mix well. Spread over the warm apple dessert. Cut into squares to serve.

Spartan

SAUCY APPLE DUMPLINGS

Ingredients for the dumplings

3 cups all-purpose flour
2 tablespoons sugar
4 teaspoons baking powder
2 teaspoons salt
1 cup vegetable shortening
3/4 cup milk
6 Golden Delicious apples, peeled, cored
2 tablespoons sugar
2 tablespoons butter or margarine
1 1/2 cups apple cider

Ingredients for the cider nutmeg sauce

1 cup apple cider
1 cup light cream
2 tablespoons sugar
1/2 teaspoon nutmeg
1/4 cup butter or margarine

Serves Six

Dumplings usually require some preparation, but Saucy Apple Dumplings are worth it. They are light and flaky and beautiful to look at, and the intense flavor of the sauce makes them good to eat as well.

Directions for the dumplings

Preheat the oven to 375 degrees. Mix the flour, 2 tablespoon sugar, baking powder and salt in a medium bowl. Cut in the shortening with a pastry blender until the mixture resembles small peas. Add the milk and mix with a fork until the mixture forms a dough. Roll into a 13x20-inch rectangle on a lightly floured surface. Cut into halves lengthwise, then into thirds crosswise, making six 6 1/2-inch squares. Place 1 apple in the center of each square. Bring the corners together to enclose the apple, pinching to seal. Place in a buttered 9x13-inch baking dish. Sprinkle with 2 tablespoons sugar and dot with the butter. Pour the apple cider around the dumplings. Bake at 375 degrees for 50 minutes or until the pastry is golden brown and the apples are tender. Spoon the Cider Nutmeg Sauce into individual serving dishes. Place 1 warm dumpling in each dish.

Directions for the cider nutmeg sauce

Combine the apple cider, cream, sugar and nutmeg in a medium saucepan. Bring to a boil and cook for 10 minutes or until the mixture is reduced to about 1 1/4 cups. Stir in the butter.

Gala

HARVEST TIME PIZZA

Ingredients for the pastry

2 cups all-purpose flour
1 tablespoon sugar
1 teaspoon salt
3/4 cup vegetable shortening
1 egg, beaten
1/4 cup ice water
1 teaspoon white vinegar

Ingredients for the topping

3 or 4 large Royal Gala or McIntosh apples, peeled, thinly sliced
1/2 cup sugar
1 teaspoon cinnamon
Salt to taste
1 1/2 cups sour cream
1 tablespoon all-purpose flour
1/2 cup firmly packed brown sugar
1/2 cup slivered blanched almonds (optional)

Serves Eight

In the sixties, when our daughter Susan was in middle school, she was invited to participate in a baking contest at the Henry Ford Museum in Greenfield Village in Dearborn, Michigan. She developed this recipe for a dessert pizza. She won a blue ribbon, much to her delight and to ours as well. We think it will delight you, too.

Directions to make the pastry

Mix the flour, sugar and salt in a bowl. Cut in the shortening until the mixture resembles large peas. Combine the egg, ice water and vinegar in a bowl and mix well. Add to the crumb mixture and stir with a fork to form a dough. Chill, wrapped, for 2 hours or longer. Press into an ungreased 15-inch pizza pan and flute the edge.

Directions to make the topping and bake the pizza

Preheat the oven to 400 degrees. Arrange the apple slices in overlapping circles over the pastry, beginning at the edge and working toward the center. Mix the sugar, 1/2 teaspoon of the cinnamon and salt in a small bowl. Sprinkle over the apples. Combine the sour cream, flour, brown sugar and the remaining 1/2 teaspoon cinnamon in a bowl and mix well. Spread evenly over the apples and sprinkle with the almonds. Bake at 400 degrees for 10 minutes. Reduce the oven temperature to 350 degrees and bake for 20 to 30 minutes longer or until the apples are tender. Cut into wedges and serve warm or at room temperature.

Fuji

A cross of Ralls Janet and Red Delicious from Japan, Fuji is a high quality variety with a long storage capability. It has very firm flesh, with a crunchy "sweet-tart" flavor great for eating fresh, in salads, or in desserts.

APPLE INDEX

MAIL ORDER FORM

The Dexter Cider Mill Apple Cookbook

Name ______________________________

Address ______________________________

City ______________ State ______________ Zip __________

Make Check payable to:

The Dexter Cider Mill, Inc.
P.O. Box 217
Chelsea, Michigan 48118

_____ Books @ $16.95 per book $__________

Shipping & Handling
$3.00 per book $__________

Total $__________

MAIL ORDER FORM

The Dexter Cider Mill Apple Cookbook

Name ______________________________

Address ______________________________

City ______________ State ______________ Zip __________

Make Check payable to:

The Dexter Cider Mill, Inc.
P.O. Box 217
Chelsea, Michigan 48118

_____ Books @ $16.95 per book $__________

Shipping & Handling
$3.00 per book $__________

Total $__________

Since 1886

DEXTER CIDER MILL INC.